At a Glance™ Series

DVD and Lesson Book

DVD Lead Guitar

Written by Andrew DuBrock, Chad Johnson & Barrett Tagliarino
Video Performers: Doug Boduch, Troy Stetina & Tom Kolb

ISBN: 978-1-4234-4299-8

HAL•LEONARD®
CORPORATION
7777 W. BLUEMOUND RD. P.O. BOX 13819 MILWAUKEE, WI 53213

Visit Hal Leonard Online at
www.halleonard.com

Table of Contents

Introduction 3

LEAD GUITAR BASICS 4

Minor Pentatonic Scale

Licks

Muting

Slides

Hammer-Ons

Pull-Offs

   "PARANOID" - Black Sabbath

   "RUNNIN' DOWN A DREAM" - Tom Petty

Bends

   "THE END" - The Beatles

   "ALL ALONG THE WATCHTOWER" - Jimi Hendrix

CHORD-TONE SOLOING 10

Basic Blues Progression

Targeting Chord Tones

Connecting The Target Notes

Real-World Chord-Tone Soloing

   "WONDERFUL TONIGHT" - Eric Clapton

   "DON'T FEAR THE REAPER" - Blue Öyster Cult

   "TIME" - Pink Floyd

   "LIVIN' ON A PRAYER" - Bon Jovi

   "SMOOTH" - Santana

BLUES ROCK LICKS 16

Blues Scale

Repetitive Licks

   "ALIVE" - Pearl Jam

   "COLD GIN" - KISS

Rhythmic Displacement

Oblique and Unison Bends

   "GIMME THREE STEPS" - Lynyrd Skynyrd

   "WHEEL IN THE SKY" - Journey

   "TIGHTROPE" - Stevie Ray Vaughn

CONNECTING PENTATONIC POSITIONS 23

Expanding the Standard Box

   "GIVE ME ONE REASON" - Tracy Chapman

   "FREE RIDE" - Edgar Winter Group

   "LA GRANGE" - ZZ Top

The Other Minor Pentatonic Shapes

Combining Several Forms

   "DREAM ON" - Aerosmith

   "RIGHTEOUS" - Eric Johnson

Introduction

Lead guitarists come in all shapes and styles: hard-core bluesmeisters like Stevie Ray Vaughan, jazz legends like Wes Montgomery, or blues-rock superstars like Eric Clapton. But what exactly makes a guitarist a lead guitar player? The concept of *lead guitar* is a bit hard to define in concrete terms. Generally, it applies to playing melodies and single notes rather than chords, but that's not always the case. Lead guitarists play parts that stand out in a song; sometimes that means playing complementary licks between a vocalist's lines, and other times that means playing a song's identifiable riff or "hook." Of course, lead guitarists also get to play all those tasty solos!

To become a proficient lead player, you have to start *playing*—not reading endless texts. If traditional method books put you to sleep, this book will wake you up and get you playing. From Hal Leonard's exciting new At a Glance series, *Lead Guitar* is presented in a snappy and fun manner intended to have you playing licks and solos in virtually no time at all. Plus, the At a Glance series uses real riffs and licks by real artists to illustrate how the concepts you're learning are applied in top-selling songs. For example, in *Lead Guitar*, you'll learn riffs and solo licks from such classics as Eric Clapton's "Wonderful Tonight," The Beatles' "The End," Pearl Jam's "Alive," and Tom Petty's "Runnin' Down a Dream," to name just a few.

Additionally, each book in the At a Glance series comes with a DVD containing video lessons that correspond to the printed material. The DVD that accompanies this book contains four video lessons, each approximately 8 to 10 minutes in length, that correspond to the topics covered in *Lead Guitar*. In these videos, lead guitar masters Doug Boduch, Troy Stetina, and Tom Kolb will show you in great detail everything from how to play your first leads to expertly connecting every pentatonic pattern on the fretboard. As you progress through *Lead Guitar*, try to play the examples first on your own, and then check out the DVD to see if you played it correctly. As the saying goes, "A picture is worth a thousand words," so be sure to use this invaluable tool on your quest to becoming a lead guitar player.

LEAD GUITAR BASICS

In this lesson, we're going to look at the basic techniques used in lead guitar playing, like slides, hammer-ons, pull-offs, and bends and we'll learn some simple, great licks in the process. Once you have these techniques under your belt, you'll also have the tools to create your own great riffs and licks.

But first, let's look at the concept of *scales*. Almost all solos or melodies are made from notes of a scale. So it makes sense that, in order to play lead guitar, you need to know some scales.

Minor Pentatonic Scale

There are a lot of different scales, but the *minor pentatonic* scale is one of the most commonly used scales in soloing, so we'll start there. The minor pentatonic is a five-note scale, which means there are five different notes before it starts to repeat again an octave higher.

We're going to be learning an A minor pentatonic scale in this lesson. Here's the most common way to play this scale. Play through this shape slowly, and concentrate on picking only one note at a time.

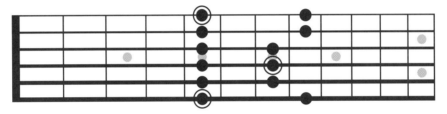

Licks

Now, most lead solos are built from *licks*, which are small phrases that can be repeated or altered. You can create some great licks with the minor pentatonic shape we just learned. Here's our first lick. It's played on the high E string.

Now let's try one that uses the B and the E strings.

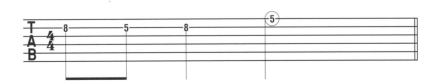

You can put these two licks together to make one larger lick, like this:

Players will usually string together a bunch of licks when playing a solo. The more licks you know, the more options you have to draw from.

Muting

Before we learn a few more licks, let's briefly cover the concept of muting. *Muting* helps keep your playing from sounding sloppy or noisy. Basically, you use the palm of your right hand to deaden the lower strings when you're not playing them.

For example, when you play a note on the third string with any finger other than your first finger, use your palm to deaden the fourth, fifth, and sixth strings so they don't rattle and make noise. Also, use your first finger to lay across the top strings behind the fretted note to keep them quiet. When you fret with your first finger, the underside of that finger should still mute the high strings.

As you move up or down the strings, continue to mute the unused strings with these methods. This way, when you're playing your solos you're only hearing what you *want* to hear!

Slides

Now let's learn a few guitar techniques that are used a lot in lead playing. The first is the *slide*. In a slide, you play one note and then slide it up to another while still holding the string down. There are two main types of slides: picked and slurred.

Let's look at the picked slide first. Pick the note, slide up, and then pick again when you reach the destination fret. Be sure to keep applying pressure with your fret-hand finger throughout.

For the slurred slide, you don't pick the string again after sliding up. When you see a slur in the music, which is the curved line connecting one note to the next, that tells you not to pick the next note.

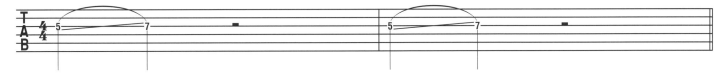

Now let's play a lick that uses both types of slides. This one starts with your third finger.

Hammer-Ons

The next technique we'll look at is the *hammer-on*. Use hammer-ons when you want to slur from a low note to a higher note on the same string.

Here's how it works: Pick the first note normally, then "hammer" onto the string at a higher fret with another finger. This will cause the higher note to sound without the need to pick it.

Remember: when you see a slur in the music, this tells you that you're not going to pick the second note.

You can perform hammer-ons with any finger combination you want. Practice all the different combinations (like first to second finger, first to third finger, etc.) to build up your finger strength.

Pull-Offs

The opposite of the hammer-on is the *pull-off*. This is what you use to slur from a high note to a lower note on the same string. The pull-off requires a little more planning than the hammer-on.

Here's how it works: You need to fret both notes at once. In the next example, we'll use our first and third fingers. After picking the first note, pull your third finger down and off the string to sound the note below (fretted with your first finger). You're in essence plucking the string by pulling off your third finger.

Again, you should practice pull-offs with all finger combinations (fourth to third finger, third to first finger, etc.)

Now let's take a look at a lick that makes use of hammer-ons *and* pull-offs.

At this point, you've already learned enough techniques to play and create some of the coolest riffs out there. Check out how Tony Iommi uses the minor pentatonic scale and hammer-ons and pull-offs in this passage from Black Sabbath's "Paranoid." Don't let those twelfth and fifteenth fret tablature markings intimidate you. Iommi's using *exactly the same minor pentatonic shape* we've been using. He just moved it up to the twelfth fret, where the shape becomes the E minor pentatonic pattern (instead of A minor pentatonic, like we've been playing).

"PARANOID"
Black Sabbath

Words and Music by Anthony Iommi, John Osbourne,
William Ward and Terence Butler

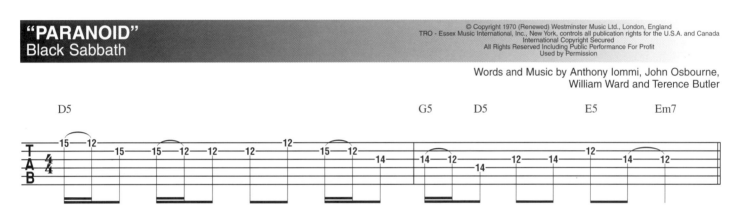

Here's another supercharged lick that Mike Campbell uses in his solo on Tom Petty's "Runnin' Down a Dream." Notice how he's using that minor pentatonic shape in the same place as Iommi did. Also check out how he repeats the same three-note combination over and over for a really slick lick. (We'll see more of these hot repetitive licks in the "Blues Rock Licks" lesson.)

"RUNNIN' DOWN A DREAM"
Tom Petty

Words and Music by Tom Petty, Jeff Lynne
and Mike Campbell

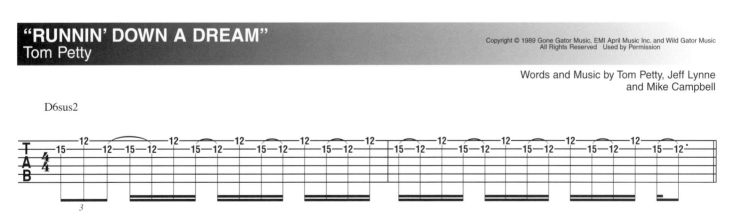

Bends

The final technique we'll learn in this lesson is the *bend*. To bend a note, you actually bend the string enough that it changes the pitch. When playing on the first, second, or third strings, most players bend by pushing up (toward the ceiling). On the fourth, fifth, and sixth strings, most players pull down to bend. For all of the bends in this lesson, we'll be pushing *up*.

Here's how it works: In the next example, we'll bend the seventh fret, third string up a whole step. To do this, put your ring finger on the seventh fret, but *also* put your index finger on the fifth fret and your middle finger on the sixth for added support. Pluck the note and push up with your ring finger, but use your other fingers to help. Check to see that you've reached your target note by playing the fifth fret of the second string. That's the note you're shooting for.

Bending takes a good amount of finger strength, so don't get discouraged if your fingers get sore. With practice, it will get easier!

You can also play half-step bends, as shown below. This time you're only bending half the distance of the previous example. Your target note is the eighth fret of the third string; play that note to check yourself.

The other two most common bends from our minor pentatonic shape start on the eighth fret of the first and second strings, like this:

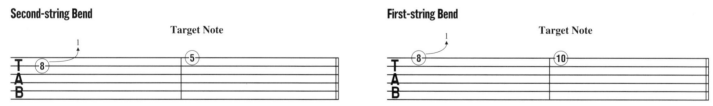

Though we've only practiced whole-step bends on the first two strings, you can play half-step bends on these strings, as well.

Now let's check out some real-world bending examples. Paul McCartney uses our very own A minor pentatonic shape with a few choice bends to kick off the solo on the Beatles' "The End." If you're wondering why that last bend says "¼" instead of "½" or "1," that's because it's a *quarter-tone* bend. Quarter-tone bends are slight bends where you push or pull the note just a little bit—somewhere between the original note and the next fret. Since you're bending up to something that's *between* two notes, you can't really check yourself with another pitch. Just bend it up a little and you'll be fine. You're just adding a little flavor to the note.

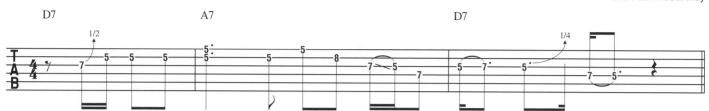

Here's another pentatonic master at work: Jimi Hendrix. He played this sweet lick in "All Along the Watchtower." Notice how here he's using the same shape, but he's starting on the ninth fret, which puts him in C♯ minor pentatonic. Did you know you'd already be soloing in *C♯ minor*?!

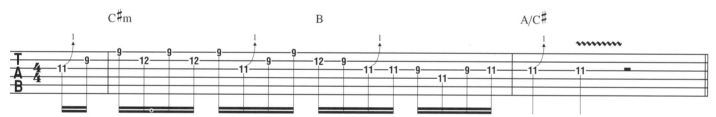

 We're going to finish this lesson up now with a mini-solo that uses a bevy of our new-found techniques: slides, hammer-ons, and pull-offs. Your fingers will get a little break here, as there are no bends. Remember to use your muting skills to keep things clean!

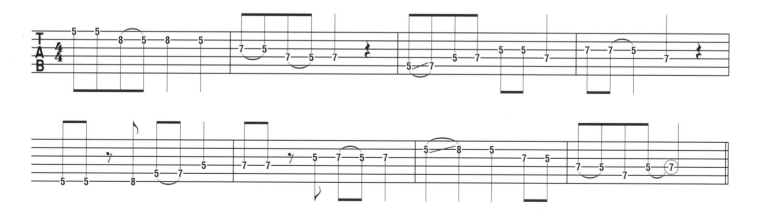

Well, you are now a legitimate lead guitarist. Welcome to the rocking world of lead guitar!

CHORD-TONE SOLOING

In this lesson we're going to learn about the basics of *chord-tone soloing*. When you take a solo in a song, the notes you choose to play over the chords can come from a general scale that fits the key of the chord progression, *or* you can use notes from each individual chord in the progression as they occur. This is chord-tone soloing. Using chord tones makes your solo fit the music more closely than using the correct scale alone.

Though this topic has unlimited potential to be as advanced as you want to take it, in this lesson we'll get you started by applying it to a basic blues progression. To make this lesson clear, the chord shapes for the rhythm part will contain exactly the same notes we'll use for the chord-tone soloing exercise. In real life, specifying the exact chord shapes won't be necessary. In fact, once you've incorporated this method into your soloing reflexes, you'll be able to imply the sound of a chord progression without a rhythm guitarist or a piano player at all! This is very useful for guitarists in a power trio setting.

Basic Blues Progression

We'll use a stripped-down blues progression in the key of A, using three major chords only: A, D, and E. To further clarify the process, we're going to keep the rhythm track at its bare bones, with no extra notes other than the ones needed to spell the three chords.

The notes in the A chord are A, C♯, and E. Play them here in fifth position.

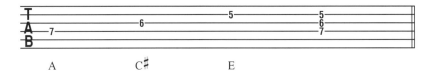

The notes in the D chord are D, F♯, and A, but for our purposes today, play the D chord with the notes inverted as shown in the graphic below (A–D–F♯). It's Ok to arrange the notes of a basic triad like this in any order. Now we can see how its notes are very close to those in the A chord. In fact, they share the A note on the seventh fret.

And the notes in an E chord are E, G♯, and B. Let's also play this chord inverted as shown (G♯–B–E), so that it's positionally close to the others. Notice that the E note on top is also shared with the A chord.

Now memorize the 12-bar blues progression so that you can remember the chord changes while we're soloing. This may take a little work, but the results will be worth it. Strum each written chord once for each beat.

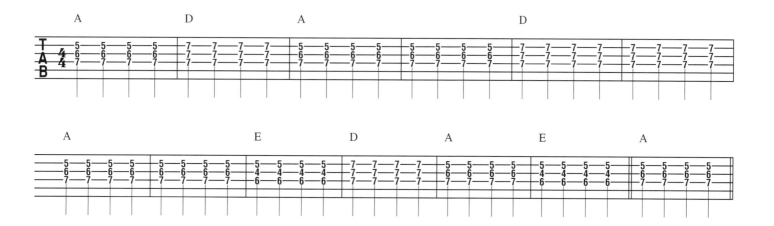

Targeting Chord Tones

Now we're going to slowly build a lead part that incorporates a particular chord tone as a target note over each chord change. We can target the root, 3rd, or 5th of each chord. Any chord tone will work, but first try using the 3rd of each chord as a target, because in most cases it's the note that differentiates a chord from the ones before and after it. This also means that if you hit one of these targets at the wrong time, you'll usually hear it right away.

Play the 3rd of each chord exactly when that chord occurs. First let's review the locations of the 3rds. The 3rd of A is C♯; the 3rd of D is F♯; and the 3rd of E is G♯.

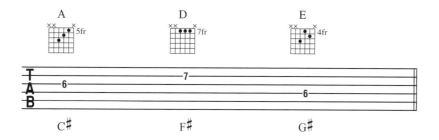

Ok, let's apply the targets to their respective chords in the progression.

Connecting the Target Notes

Now that we know the locations and timing of our targets, let's apply them in conjunction with the correct scale to fit the chords. In the blues genre, the most commonly used scale, and the one we'll use to connect our chord tones, is the minor pentatonic scale. We just learned this scale in the "Lead Guitar Basics" lesson, but let's review it again, just to make sure it's under our fingers.

A minor Pentatonic Scale

We insert a neighboring scale tone one beat before each chord-tone target. Before the C♯ target on string 3, use C at the fifth fret or D at the 7th fret; before the F♯ target on string 2, use F at fret 6 or G at fret 8; and approach the G♯ target on string 4 from below with a G note or from above with the A note at fret 7.

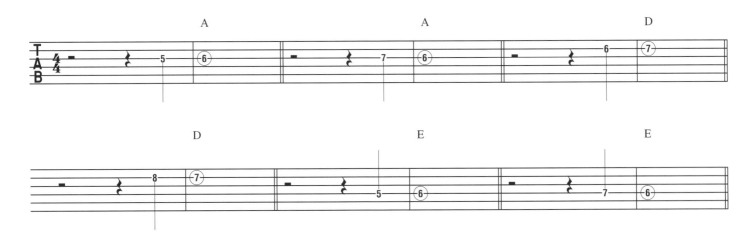

Alright! Let's play it with the chord progression.

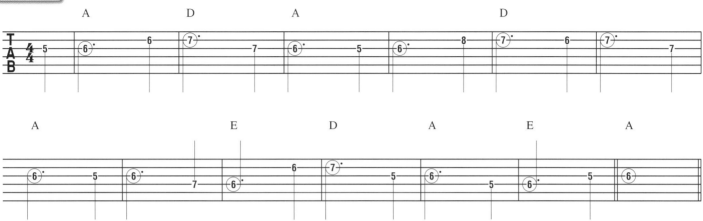

From here it's a matter of practice to incorporate the target chord tones into longer groups of notes and within other licks. Remember to focus on adding notes before the targets—not after—and make sure you hit the targets on time, right when the chord change occurs.

This next example leads into the 3rd with two scalar-approaching eighth notes, then follows the target with the root of the chord.

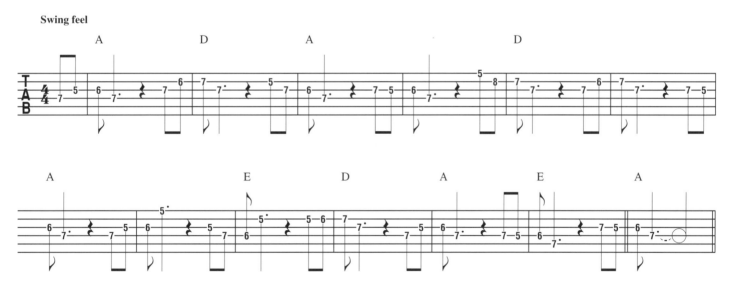

Of course, in actual music the rhythms and notes are rarely this deliberate or repetitive, but it's a good way to train your ear to hear the effects of using chord tones. With enough practice, it'll become second nature and you'll be able to incorporate this idea into any solo you want.

Real-World Chord-Tone Soloing

Now that we know how to create our own chord-tone solos, let's check out how a few hot-shot guitarists have incorporated chord tones into their solos and licks.

First off is Eric Clapton, playing the classic riff to "Wonderful Tonight." In this example, notice how he takes a lick and adapts it to end with a chord tone over each chord (A, the 5th of D/F♯; E, the 3rd of C/E; and D, the 5th of G). Sandwiched in the middle of the final phrase is that D chord. Here he starts with a chord tone (A, the 5th) and continues with a line that ends on a chord tone (D, the 5th) of the G chord in the following measure. Since Clapton is modifying a phrase each time, this also means that he's not approaching the chord tones from a half step above or below, like we've been doing. Clapton also uses another common trick: anticipating the chord changes. Notice how he hits many of those chord tones one eighth note *before* the chord change.

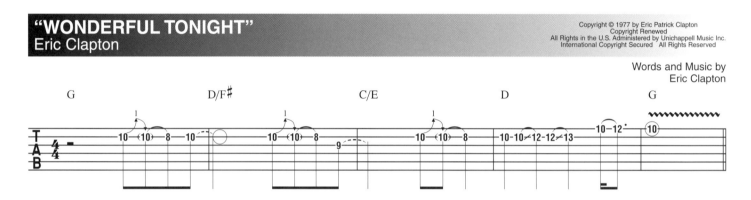

"WONDERFUL TONIGHT"
Eric Clapton

Words and Music by
Eric Clapton

Our next one comes from Blue Öyster Cult's "Don't Fear the Reaper" (no cowbell allowed!). This lick tastefully riffs between vocal phrases, perfectly filling in the space. The first chord tone (E, 5th of A5) touches only for a second before popping down to anticipate the G chord with a B (3rd). Again, that F6/9 chord is anticipated with the A (3rd), and the following G is also anticipated with a G note (root). Then, the next A5 chord is anticipated by a half beat (the A, root). At this point, the A note is held through the G, all through the next F6/9 chord, where it also functions as a chord tone (the 3rd).

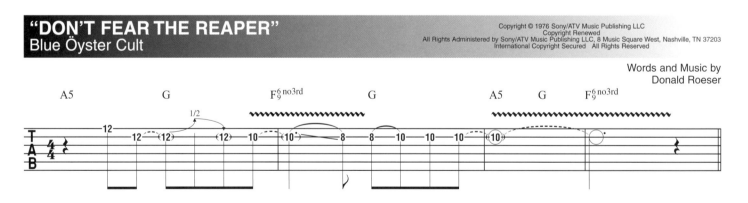

"DON'T FEAR THE REAPER"
Blue Öyster Cult

Words and Music by
Donald Roeser

In Pink Floyd's "Time," David Gilmour pulls off some licks that use multiple chord tones for each chord. Notice how he hits *almost* every note in the Dmaj7 chord (F♯, A, and C♯—everything but the root). For the following Amaj7 and Dmaj7 chords, check out how he uses the completely opposite approach to anticipation; here, he waits a second before resolving to a chord tone—E (5th) for the Amaj7 and F♯ (3rd) for the Dmaj7. Then, he finishes by nailing the third (C♯) for the final Amaj7 chord.

"TIME"
Pink Floyd

Words and Music by Roger Waters, Nicholas Mason,
David Gilmour and Rick Wright

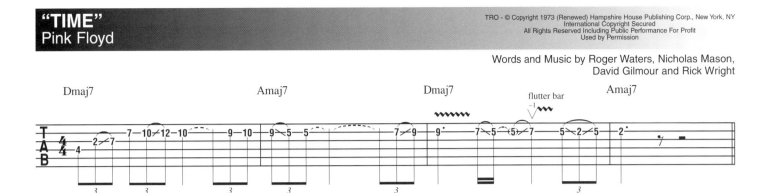

In Bon Jovi's "Livin' on a Prayer," guitarist Richie Sambora starts his solo by anticipating a chord tone for each chord change.

"LIVIN' ON A PRAYER"
Bon Jovi

Words and Music by Jon Bon Jovi, Desmond Child
and Richie Sambora

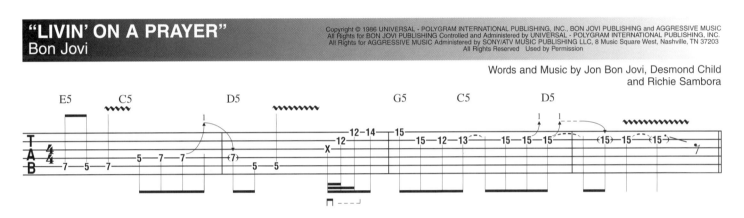

Another solo master, Carlos Santana, shows his chord-tone soloing stuff on his duet with Rob Thomas, "Smooth." Check out how he uses a chord tone on every chord change—*even when the chord changes underneath a held note*! For example, he's holding that A note for the Am and F chords, but it functions as a chord tone for both chords (the root for Am and the 3rd for F). On the final E7 chord, he hits the 7th (D), and follows that up with the root (E).

"SMOOTH"
Rob Thomas

Words by Rob Thomas
Music by Rob Thomas and Itaal Shur

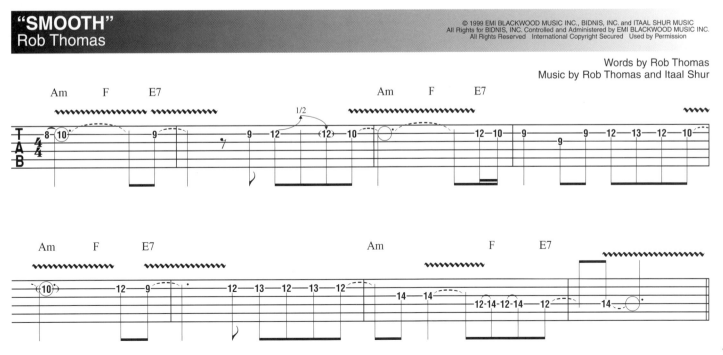

BLUES ROCK LICKS

Since the beginning, rock music has been a close cousin to the blues, so it makes sense that guitarists would borrow from the blues when coming up with rock licks. The result's been a large vocabulary of licks that share qualities from both genres, and that's what we're going to be studying in this lesson. As you'll see, these licks find themselves at home across all styles of rock—whether it's the southern rock of Lynyrd Skynyrd, the contemporary rock of Pearl Jam, the pop rock of Journey, or the rockin' blues of Stevie Ray Vaughan.

Blues Scale

A good percentage of these licks make use of the good old *blues scale*. If you're not familiar with that one, here's the common shape known as the "box position" in the key of A.

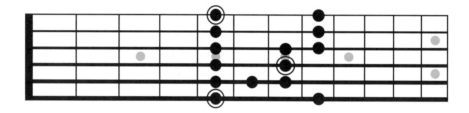

We'll go ahead and work exclusively in the key of A to keep things simple, but remember: any lick that doesn't contain an open string can be transposed to any key just by moving it around the neck.

This scale sounds so good, you can literally just run straight down it and end up with a great lick.

Since it's a six-note scale, triplets work great as well.

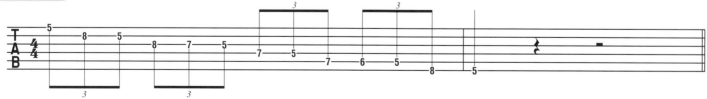

Repetitive Licks

One of the common uses of the blues scale is the *repetitive lick*. You can take a small fragment of the scale and create fast, exciting licks that add intensity to your solos. Maybe something like this:

Here's another really common one that uses a bend:

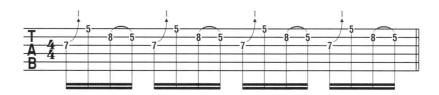

A variation on this lick uses sixteenth-note triplets, like this:

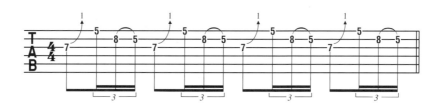

Let's check this one out in a real-world situation. Here we have Mike McCready riffing off of it in his solo for Pearl Jam's "Alive." Note how he's slid the pattern up to the twelfth fret, where he's now playing in E. Also check out how he's sped up the pull-off, and it throws the rhythm for a cool loop.

"ALIVE"
Pearl Jam

Music by Stone Gossard
Lyric by Eddie Vedder

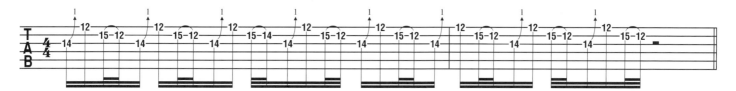

You can also sequence a pattern up or down through the strings. Say you start off with this lick:

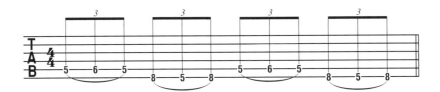

You can repeat this same little motif on each set of strings in the scale shape. You might come up with something like this:

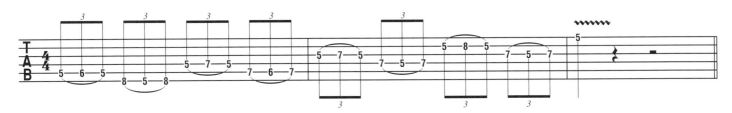

Or let's say you start off with the first repetitive lick we learned (see page 17). You could repeat that idea moving down through the strings and get something like this:

Now let's check this out in a real-world tune. Kiss' "Cold Gin" features a perfect repetitive lick as a fill during the second chorus. Again, this lick uses the E minor pentatonic scale in the twelfth position. The initial idea uses a sixteenth-note triplet on the first string, followed by an eighth note on the second string. The lick continues on the second string, and so on.

"COLD GIN"
KISS

Words and Music by
Ace Frehley

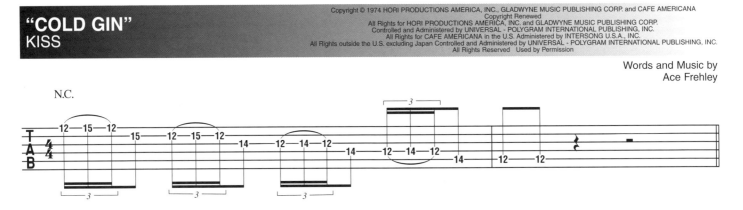

Rhythmic Displacement

Don't forget that most of these licks can be made to sound fresh by using *rhythmic displacement*. If you take a repeating sixteenth-note lick and move it over within the beat by one sixteenth note, it will have a different effect.

Let's demonstrate with the first repetitive lick we learned (turn back to page 17 to refresh your memory). We're going to move the entire lick back by one sixteenth note, so that the second note of the lick, the G note, will be on the downbeat.

If we do the same thing again, the E note will appear on the downbeat, like this:

And the last variation puts the E♭ note on the downbeat. This one sounds a bit meaner than the others, because it's really accenting that blues note.

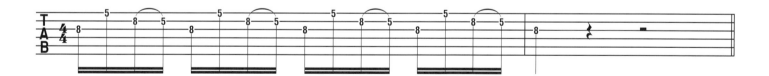

So if you keep this concept in mind, you'll more than double the amount of repetitive licks you know, because every time you learn one, it'll produce three or four variations.

Oblique and Unison Bends

Bends of all types are used throughout the blues rock style, but two types have appeared over and over: *oblique bends* and *unison bends*.

An oblique bend occurs when you bend a note and sound it against a note on another string that's not bent. This has a southern rock feel to it and was used extensively by bands like Lynyrd Skynyrd, but also by players like Jimmy Page and Eric Clapton as well. Here's a classic example:

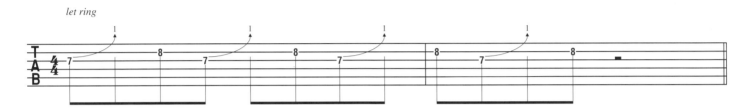

You can also play a similar lick on the B and E strings in the same box position.

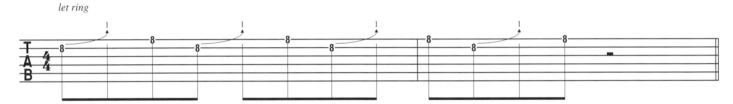

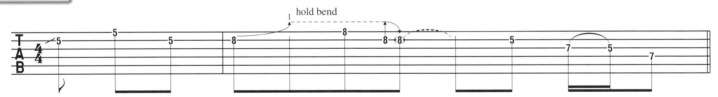

You'll see these bends used in all types of licks, like this one:

Or this one:

Here's a lick that you can repeat for as long as you like. It lasts the length of three eighth notes, so it keeps starting on different parts of the measure each time.

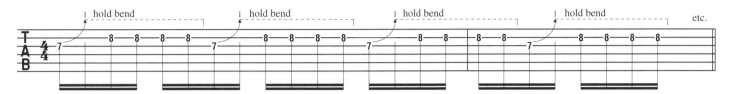

For a real-world example of a similar oblique bend, let's go to one of the masters: Lynyrd Skynyrd. In this excerpt from "Gimme Three Steps," check out how both the bend and the other note are played at the same time. Also, notice how the lick eases up to that full bend by not bending up the whole way at first. Likewise, the bend takes its time releasing from the bend midway through the measure, dropping slightly before picking up again. Gradually bending up to and releasing bends like these is always a nifty trick!

"GIMME THREE STEPS"
Lynyrd Skynyrd

Words and Music by Allen Collins
and Ronnie Van Zant

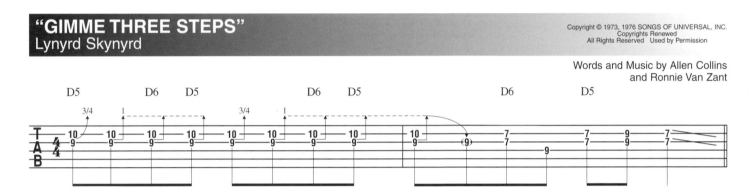

For a unison bend, you're bending a note on one string up to the same note on a higher string. It looks like this:

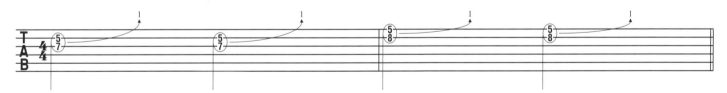

These have a nice, gritty sound that Hendrix and Clapton used quite a bit with licks like this:

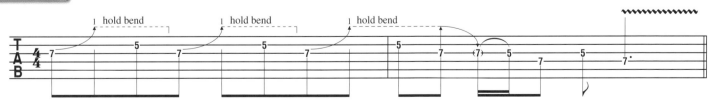

Another common approach with unison bends is to move up the scale on one string and play a unison bend for each note on the string below it. For example, here we'll move up the A minor pentatonic scale on the B string and bend on the G string from a whole step below each time.

Let's finish this lesson by checking out some unison bends in action. Here's Neal Schon playing some mean unison bends at the end of Journey's "Wheel in the Sky:"

"WHEEL IN THE SKY"
Journey

Words and Music by Robert Fleischman, Neal Schon
and Diane Valory

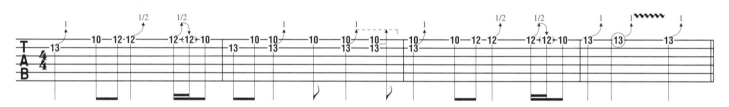

Finally, blues master Stevie Ray Vaughan tears up his heavy strings with a fierce unison bend on this excerpt from his solo on "Tightrope:"

"TIGHTROPE"
Stevie Ray Vaugan

Written by Stevie Ray Vaughan and
Doyle Bramhall

CONNECTING PENTATONIC POSITIONS

Are you getting tired of your same old box position pentatonic licks? Do you stare in awe when you see players like Eric Johnson or Joe Perry span the entire fretboard in one seamless lick? Well, fret no more; your troubles are over! In this lesson we're going to concentrate on breaking that position-playing barrier that so many pentatonic players have trouble with. It's been a good home, but it's time to say "goodbye"—or at least, "see ya later"—to the good old pentatonic box shape.

Expanding the Standard Box

Before we step into completely new territory, we're going to get our feet wet by expanding the standard box shape. We learned the standard box-shape pentatonic scale in the "Lead Guitar Basics" lesson, but let's take a look at it again to refresh our memory.

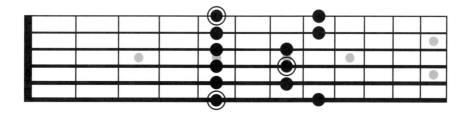

We'll work in A throughout this lesson for simplicity, but be sure to practice what you learn in all twelve keys.

Lower Extension Shape

Ok, most of us know this shape like the back of our hand. But if this is the extent of your fretboard travels, you're missing out. It's a great big neck out there. Let's look at our first extension of this shape. All we're going to do is add two frets on the lower two strings. It looks like this:

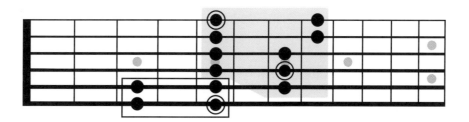

Notice that this brings a shift of position into the scale. Don't be afraid of this! Shifts are essential in gaining freedom across the fretboard. Also notice that we only added one note to this scale: the low G. The C note on the third fret of the fifth string is the same note as the C note on the eighth fret of the sixth string (part of the pentatonic box).

Let's check out how this extension works in a few licks. Here's our first example. Notice how we use a slide to shift positions into the lower extension shape. This is a really common method that you'll see over and over.

Here's one that's kind of funky.

This lower extended shape should feel familiar to you already and here's the reason: those four notes on the fifth and sixth strings are the same notes and make up the same shape as the four notes on the fourth and third strings.

Upper Extension Shape

Ok, now let's check out another extension to the standard pattern—this time on the top end. This shape involves the top three strings and is sometimes called the "Albert King box," because many players cop his legendary blues licks in this position.

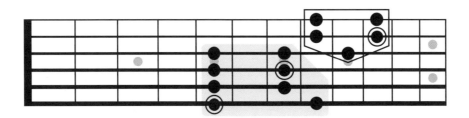

There are several different ways to shift to the upper extension, so experiment to see what you like best. You could shift with your first finger, by sliding up from the fifth fret to the seventh fret of the third string. Or, you could shift with your third finger by sliding up from the seventh fret to the ninth fret of the third string. You could even shift with your second finger, by using it to play the seventh fret of the third string (instead of your third finger), and then sliding up to the ninth fret with this finger. Depending on the lick, you may end up using all the options at one time or another, so it's good to practice them all.

Speaking of licks, let's check out this shape in action.

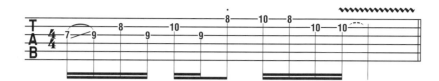

Again we see the use of the slide to shift positions. And here's another one using this shape. This one contains a classic move at the end of the first measure: a slide up to the ninth fret of the third string and the following two eighth notes. You'll hear that move drawn out and repeated all the time.

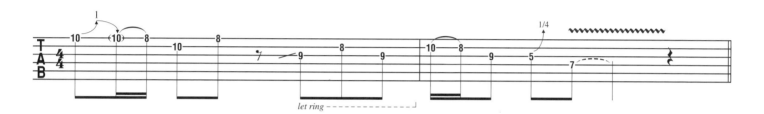

This extended shape on its own is enough to play countless solos and licks. Here are a few tried and true examples. The first one comes from the opening measures of the guitar solo on Tracy Chapman's "Give Me One Reason." There are only two notes in the box shape before the slide to the upper extension, but the lick hangs out there for the rest of this excerpt.

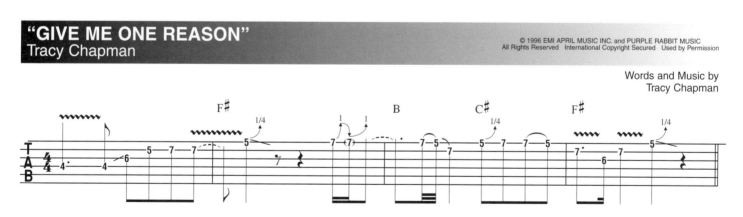

"GIVE ME ONE REASON"
Tracy Chapman

Words and Music by
Tracy Chapman

This guitar solo from Edgar Winter Group's "Free Ride" features some tasty bends in the pentatonic box, but a quick slide to the upper extension allows for the slick bend at the end.

Words and Music by
Dan Hartman

"FREE RIDE"
Edgar Winter Group

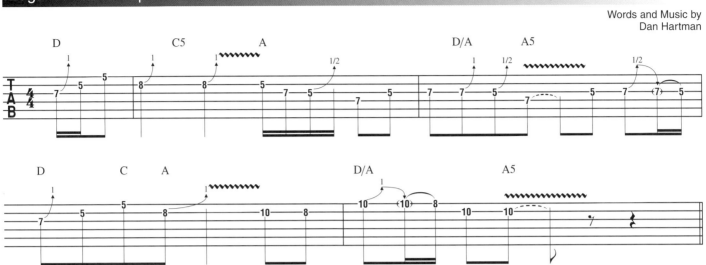

This excerpt, from ZZ Top's "La Grange," uses both the lower and upper extensions. Check out how it eases into things by starting down on that lower extension, then moves up to the box shape in the second measure and follows with a huge slide to that upper extension at the beginning of measure 6. Midway through the seventh measure, another slide takes things back to the standard box shape, where this lick finishes off.

"LA GRANGE"
ZZ Top

Words and Music by Billy F Gibbons, Dusty Hill
and Frank Lee Beard

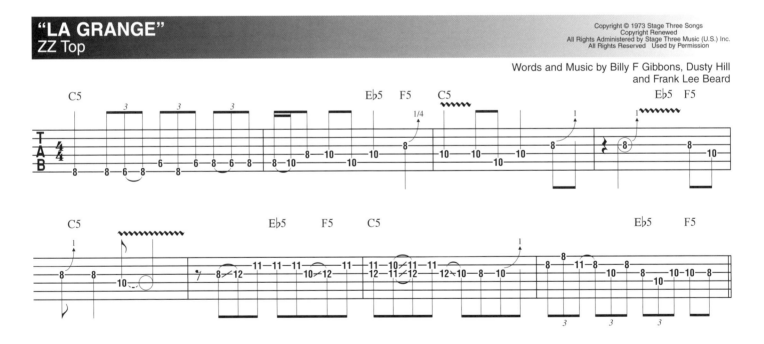

The Other Minor Pentatonic Shapes

Ok, now that you've tested the waters, it's time to jump in. There are five scale forms for the minor pentatonic on the guitar neck. You already know one of them: the standard box position, which we'll call Scale Form 1. It's time to learn the other four in order to allow you true fretboard freedom. Again, these are all presented in A minor, but be sure to transpose them to all keys.

Scale Form 2

First up is Scale Form 2. You should recognize the top few strings of this shape—they're from the upper extension shape you just learned.

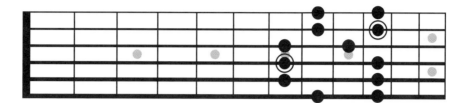

Here's a bluesy lick that uses this form:

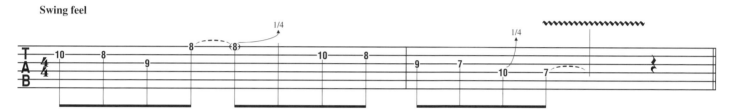

Don't neglect those quarter-step bends. They really add to the flavor of licks like these. Here's another funky one that works the lower strings of this shape. Watch for the dead notes! I'm picking the string, but not applying full pressure with my fret hand.

Combining Forms 1 and 2

Ok, now let's take a look at some licks that combine forms 1 and 2. This example uses both ascending and descending slides to make the position changes.

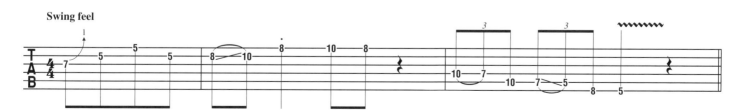

In this slow blues lick, we use *octave transference* when shifting positions, meaning we play the same thing and octave lower.

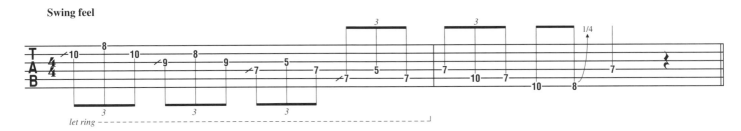

Scale Form 3

All right, let's learn our next scale form: number 3. It looks like this:

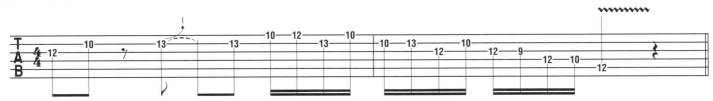

The upper portion of this shape is used quite often. Here's an example using this form. We start off with a really common bend from this form and then go into a quick descending sequence.

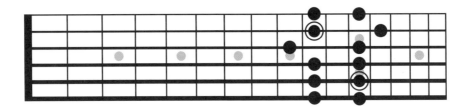

Combining Forms 2 and 3

Now let's combine forms 2 and 3 in a few licks. This example makes repeated use of slides for a smooth, slippery sound.

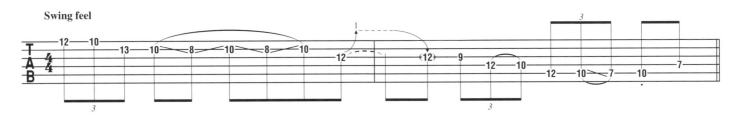

This next one is slightly reminiscent of Hendrix. With its hammered double stops shifting rather abruptly back and forth between the positions, it'll really test your familiarity with the two scale forms.

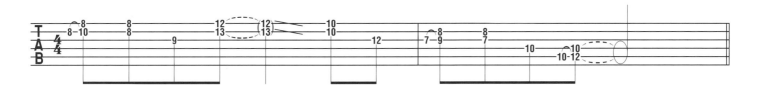

Scale Form 4

Next we come to Scale Form 4. Be careful with this one, since it most closely resembles the standard box position.

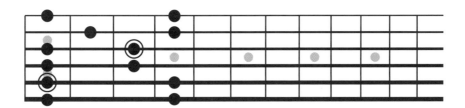

There are several classic moves in this form as well. This lick makes use of an oblique bend that you've probably heard thousands of times. Listen to be sure you're getting the whole-step bend in tune for the oblique bend.

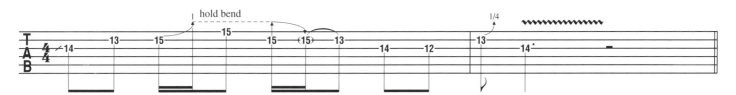

You'll certainly recognize this blues cliché:

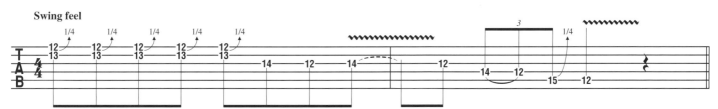

Combining Forms 3 and 4

Now we'll combine forms 3 and 4 and see what we can come up with. This one is slightly reminiscent of Clapton during his Cream years. Notice the slides used to move down in position and then back up as well.

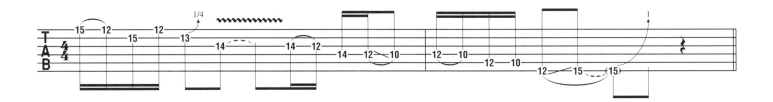

Scale Form 5

Finally, we come to the last form: Scale Form 5. You'll recognize the low strings from the lower extension shape we learned in the beginning. It looks like this:

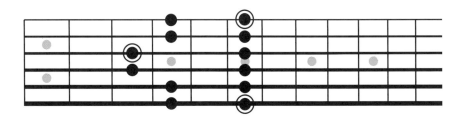

This shape sees a good deal of blues action. You might hear things like this:

Swing feel

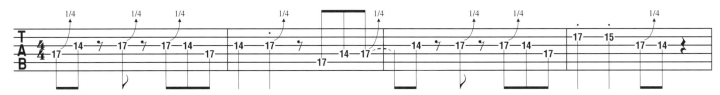

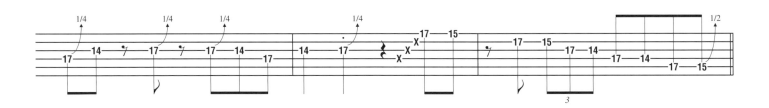

Now we'll combine Scale Forms 4 and 5. You *might* recognize the beginning of this one.

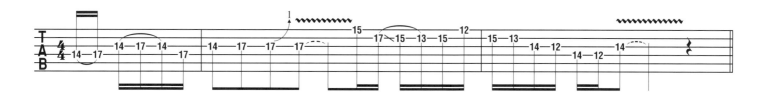

Combining Several Forms

All right, we've been through all the forms now and have combined two at a time to show you how it can be done. Now it's time to take the plunge and link several forms together in a single lick.

These final examples will make use of slides as well as more abrupt shifts to navigate through the forms. The key is being very comfortable with all five forms and being able to visualize them all over the neck.

Here's one that slides its way up through all the forms using the top two strings. Take care with those slides so you don't over shoot. Some slides are two frets and some are three.

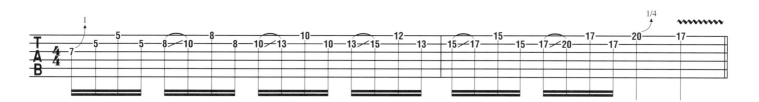

Here's one that's in the style of Eric Johnson. If there's anyone that knows how to connect pentatonic positions, it's Eric. Every time we move up to the next position, a slide is involved.

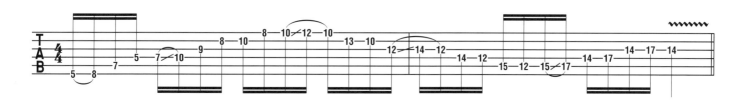

This example is truly one of those neck-spanning licks—it covers over a full three-octave span. Be very careful of the fingering for this one. You're not staying in any one form for more than three notes.

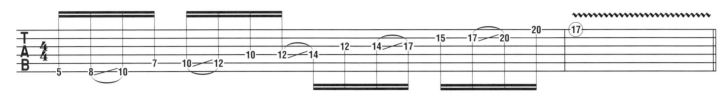

Now let's check out some of the masters at work as they move fluidly throughout these shapes. The first one features a Joe Perry lick from Aerosmith's classic hit "Dream On." Here, he starts in the box position, slides up to the upper extension, and then jumps way up to Scale Form 4 to close things out.

"DREAM ON"
Aerosmith

Words and Music by
Steven Tyler

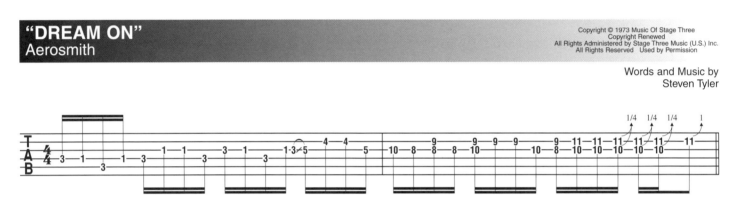

Here's Eric Johnson seamlessly moving from Pattern 1 down to Pattern 4 in "Righteous." Check out how he reaches up to the seventeenth fret in the first measure, instead of going up to the thirteenth fret of the second string. Since the frets are closer together up here, it's easier to make this stretch than to play consecutive notes on the same fret.

"RIGHTEOUS"
Eric Johnson

By Eric Johnson

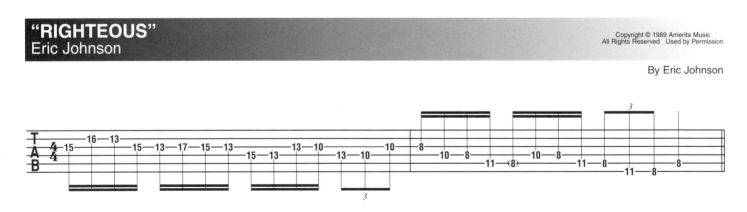

Your homework is to write twenty more licks! You should be armed with the tools to navigate the entire fretboard at this point, so put that knowledge to use and come up with your own neck-spanning licks. Good luck!